Language Lessons *for* Children

by Kathy Weitz

Primer One

Teaching Helps

for Autumn, Winter, & Spring

Preface

When I began educating my children at home more than two decades ago, one of the first books I read was *For the Children's Sake* by Susan Schaeffer Macaulay. Here I was formally introduced to the philosophies of Charlotte Mason, a Victorian education reformer. In my girlhood, L. M. Montgomery had given me a first glimpse of similar methods via *Anne of Avonlea*, so Charlotte Mason's ideas immediately attracted me. Later, I read her complete series on education which provided additional insight and encouragement. After all these years and after teaching many students of all ages (my own and others), I continue to consider many of her methods ideal for teaching young children and the perfect preparation for a rigorous classical education later.

All of the ideas and methods contained in the *Language Lessons for Children* series have been field tested and honed in several educational settings with students of differing ages, abilities, and learning styles. The primary testers have been my own five sons and one daughter in our homeschool classroom.

Language Lessons for Children is a work of "heart". It is the series I wish I had had when my children were young. It is the result of much trial and error on my part. I pray that it will provide structure, simplicity, and much delight for those tasked with the instruction of young students in our extraordinary English language.

~kpw
Soli Deo Gloria!
April, 2014

Acknowledgements

Although my name is on the cover, the Primer series in many ways has been a collaborative effort. I owe a great debt of gratitude to many folks. The gorgeous cover designs are the craftsmanship of my friend Jayme Metzgar, with image credit to The Graphics Fairy (www.thegraphicsfairy.com). Many other friends have helped with both editing and content: in particular, Kimberlynn Curles, Emily Cook, Cheryl Turner, Karen Gill, Carolyn Vance, Lene Jaqua, and the exceptional teachers, moms, and students of Providence Preparatory Academy. And of course, the main source of help and encouragement in myriad ways—from design consultation to field testing to dinner duty—has come from my dear husband and my wonderful children.

~kpw

PRIMER ONE TEACHING HELPS
CONTENTS

Primer One Spring Teaching Notes & Helps

Appendix

INTRODUCTION

My heart overflows with a pleasing theme;
I address my verses to the king;
my tongue is like the pen of a ready scribe.
~ Psalm 45:1, ESV

All Language Lessons at Cottage Press aim to develop *ready scribes* who pen *pleasing themes* flowing from a heart of truth, goodness, and beauty. The *Primer* series is designed to provide gentle yet meaningful lessons for early elementary students in preparation for more rigorous grammar and composition instruction in late elementary, middle, and high school.

Weekly copybook and narration selections are drawn from classic children's literature and poetry. These time-proven imitation methods fill students' minds with a ready supply of elegant and beautiful words and patterns of expression, and equip their imaginations with a delightful treasury of stories. Nature and art study lessons included each week also provide "scope for the imagination", and hone the students' powers of observation, description, and attention to detail—necessary attributes for *ready scribes*.

Primer books are sequential in skills: *Primer One Autumn, Primer One Winter,* and *Primer One Spring* followed by *Primer Two Autumn, Primer Two Winter,* and *Primer Two Spring.* Familiarity with the concepts from the preceding book is assumed, but the lessons are so straightforward that students may begin at their current skill level.

Students beginning *Primer One* should have achieved

beginning spelling and phonics proficiency, be ready for beginning chapter books, and be able to copy words and sentences. Students beginning *Primer Two* should have achieved intermediate spelling and phonics proficiency, be able to read beginning chapter books with basic fluency, and be able to copy sentences and short paragraphs. *Primer One* is very generally appropriate for 2nd to 3rd grade students, and *Primer Two* for 3rd to 4th grade students, but both could be used very effectively by older students as well.

℘ LESSON FORMAT

Each *Primer* book is divided into twelve weeks of study. Each week is divided into four days' work, with a poetry or prose selection at its heart. Each day's lesson includes a short copybook exercise from the copybook selection and a brief grammar or phonics review exercise connected with the copybook selection. The weekly routine also includes narration exercises on Days 1 and 3, a nature study lesson on Day 2, and a picture study lesson on Day 4. Detailed directions for each of these lesson components is provided in the Pedagogy & Practice section below.

℘ LESSON PREPARATION

The lessons in this book are designed to free teachers from as much preparation work as possible. For the most part, you will just open to the week's lesson and begin. Additional preparation may be necessary if you opt to add the enrichment ideas included *Teaching Helps*, but even that preparation is minimal.

Pedagogy & Practice

☙ Copybook

The method is simple: students copy a worthy copybook selection—a poem, a psalm, a hymn, or a prose passage. They carefully reproduce the text of the copybook selection in their best handwriting with proper spelling, punctuation, and capitalization. In *Primer One*, space is provided in the student workbook for each copybook assignment. In *Primer Two*, students complete copybook assignments in a separate composition book dedicated to the purpose.

Copybook sessions should be no longer than ten minutes for most students. Some students will need even shorter sessions in the beginning. If necessary, divide the copybook selection into several parts and complete the work over two or three sessions during the day. It is better to complete only a portion of the copybook selection in an excellent manner than to slog through the entire thing in a sloppy manner. If a student really struggles, begin by requiring only a single sentence. Require an incremental amount more in each subsequent lesson until the student is able to complete the entire selection in one sitting.

Before students begin copying, spend a few minutes together reading and examining the copybook selection. Point out the punctuation and capitalization. Discuss any words that might be difficult to spell. Instruct students to use their best handwriting and to copy each letter and punctuation mark accurately.

At the end of each copybook session, have students compare

what they have written with the original. If they have made mistakes and do not catch them this way, go through the copybook selection with them word by word. Is each word spelled correctly? Is each capital letter and punctuation mark reproduced correctly? If need be, go letter by letter through words they have misspelled. This process may seem tedious, but it will prove invaluable to students trained by it to catch their own mistakes. Some students will need help to focus on specific and small details continuously. Do not hesitate to give students this kind of help. Independence will come eventually as they consistently practice a habit of attention to detail.

A NOTE ABOUT POETRY COPYBOOK ~ For poetry copybook selections, have students align the verses to the left, since it is difficult to center handwritten lines. The daily copybook selections are left-aligned for this reason. In *Primer One*, poems at the beginning of a week are centered for aesthetic reasons.

A NOTE ABOUT SCRIPTURE COPYBOOK SELECTIONS ~ *Primer* copybook selections are taken from the New King James version of the Bible. In general, the King James Version is preferable for language lessons because of its incomparable language patterns and expressiveness. Familiarity with the King James style is vital for our students because so many important literary, theological, and political works employ this style. However, because the *Primer* student is still learning basic spelling, grammar, and word usage conventions, it is prudent to offer the New King James version for this level. The New King James retains much of the beauty and form of the King James, but updates the verb and pronoun forms, along with other grammar features.

A Note About Names Referring to the Trinity ~ *Primer* copybook selections follow the convention of capitalizing pronouns that refer to the persons of the Trinity. Some translators and theologians do not follow this convention, so if you prefer that students not capitalize these words, just make the change in the text.

ℭℛ Dictation

On Day 4 of each week, students write a portion of the copybook selection from dictation. For students who are new to both copybook and dictation, do a bit of both. Start by dictating a single sentence, then have students copy another sentence or two.

Allow students to study the copybook selection before you begin to dictate. Point out capitalization and punctuation features. Go over the spelling of any words that could give trouble. You may even give hints reminding students of the capitalization, punctuation, and spelling details as you dictate. Tell students exactly what they need to know at each word, each punctuation mark. Spell difficult words on the board where they can see them.

Gradually increase the length of the dictation selection and decrease the number of helps and hints you give. As students advance, adjust the challenge level by increasing the speed of dictation and decreasing the number of repetitions you give.

Students should eventually be able to take dictation without any help or hints, but this takes time and patience. Some students will be faster at achieving this goal than others.

Do not worry if students continue to need help through this series.

ℭ℞ SPELLING, GRAMMAR, AND WORD USAGE

Lessons on most days include a short spelling or grammar exercise drawn from the daily copybook. This is intended to supplement, not replace, the students' other phonics and spelling studies. The importance of systematic and thorough phonics instruction in the elementary years cannot be overstated. My own preferred approach for phonics instruction is that which Romalda Spalding developed in *The Writing Road for Reading*. There are several excellent curricula available based on this approach. See the *Primer Resources Webpage* for links to suggested resources.

The majority of these lessons are self-explanatory, but notes and answer keys are provided in the following pages as the activities warrant.

Whenever students are instructed to write or copy words, have them read back to you what they have written, *exactly* as written. Have them make corrections as needed at this point. This is a very important step for students, as it both reinforces correct spelling and promotes editing skills.

ℭ℞ READING AND NARRATION

Twice a week, you will read a short fable or narrative with students, and they will narrate it back to you. The ability to clearly articulate a story is a foundational skill required for virtually every type of writing: essays, research reports, legal documents. Students must learn to recall a story sequentially as well as discern its most important parts. Many children are natural storytellers and enjoy this greatly. You will need access to the classic children's book from which the narratives for each *Primer* are drawn. See the Required Materials section in each *Primer* for the book needed to accomapny the particular workbook you are using.

Narration is meant to be a simple process. Prepare students for the copybook selection by reviewing the listed vocabulary words and explaining the meanings as needed in very simple terms.

For younger students, read the narrative aloud, then ask them to tell you the story. Many students will need no prompting at all. Some students may need a bit of help getting started. For example, you may write on the board the names of the main characters in order of appearance as a subtle reminder of the sequence. The vocabulary words may also be helpful for this purpose.

Students who are advancing in their reading skills may be able to read all or part of the copybook selection aloud to you. For these students, it is still best to alternate the initial reading method. Read one day's selection to them, then allow them to read the next day's selection on their own so that they gain practice in listening as well as reading skills regularly.

The best way to teach students to narrate is to model it yourself. Read a story aloud and narrate it to them afterwards. This will help you to see the challenges they will face in narration. You may even find that this is a skill you need to work on.

After students have narrated back to you orally, they may draw a picture or a series of pictures in the space provided to illustrate the story.

ℛ Nature Study

Regular nature walks with students are a must. Give your young students plenty of opportunity for first-hand observation and tactile experience with the natural world. Fresh air, sunshine, and exercise for all of you are the healthy side benefits.

Nature study at this age should rely mostly on the student's own observations, but if your physical location makes that difficult or impossible, you may also need to pick up some books from the library or use online resources.

The nature study exercises are fairly self-explanatory. Students observe, draw, or collect (if possible) a nature specimen from your yard or a nearby park. Notes on each week's nature study lesson are provided in the *Teaching Notes and Helps* section of this book. In some cases you will read a short selection from this section to students and/or view resources at the *Primer Resources Webpage*, linked from the Cottage Press website, *cottagepress.net*.

Keep nature study brief and simple. Delighting in God's creation is as much a goal of nature study as learning to learning to identify and classify. When you go on a nature walk, take along a sketch pad. Make quick sketches and notes of what you observe. Bring back specimens if at all possible, so students can take their time for a more complete and careful drawing.

14

Start a collection of field guides, and bookmark helpful websites for nature identification. The *Primer Resources Webpage* has links to websites and resources to get you started.

℘ PICTURE STUDY

Picture study sharpens students' powers of observation. It forms a sense of beauty. It teaches students discernment and appreciation of true quality in art. Students study each artist's work for a period of six weeks, in order that they may become familiar with that artist's particular style.

Choose two artists to accompany each *Primer* book. You will need to print out the six works by each artist you have chosen. Cottage Press provides free downloadable PDF documents for a variety of well-known artists whose works will appeal to younger students. Each picture is copyrighted, as per the person or museum who owns it. These cannot be sold as a printed book, but the copyright allows for you to print them in the size you need.

Each Picture Study PDF also provides you with a few biographical notes on the artists that you may mention to students. However, the primary goal at this age is for the students to observe and describe.

Allow students a few minutes to quietly observe the painting. Tell them to try to remember as many details as possible. Then hide the picture and ask them to tell you what they saw. You may need to offer a little help to get them started: "There was a big cow in the center of the picture. What surrounded it?" Do not explain the picture to them. Give just enough help that they can take over on their own. They may want to describe the picture orally or in writing, or they may want to sketch it from memory.

Many students will need a little practice to do this well. In a classroom or co-op setting, allow the youngest students to go first, and then ask the others to give additional details. Students quickly realize that they must look for lots of details so that they will have something to add. If you are working one-on-one with a student, you may need to help by taking turns describing one detail each. As in the narration exercises, model the process of observation and description.

Below are a few questions you can use as prompts. These begin to introduce some art terminology in a gentle and natural manner that actually makes the task of description easier.

- What part of the picture is your eye immediately drawn towards?
- How did the artist draw your eye there?
- What do you see in the foreground?
- What do you see in the background?
- Where is the light coming from in this picture? (Observe the shadows and light spots.)

After students have observed and described the painting, have them do their best to reproduce it in the space provided using high-quality colored pencils. Alternately, you can print out the picture and have them cut and paste it in the space. A few blank lines are included at the bottom of each picture study page. Students should copy the title of the picture and the name of the artist with the year the artwork was produced.

See links to resources for further study at the *Primer Resources Webpage*. Find books about the artist you are studying. Look for additional works by the artist. Check to see if your local art museum has any of the artist's works in its gallery.

WEEKLY ROUTINE

"Habit is either the best of servants or the worst of masters." ~ Nathanael Emmons

Routine (habit) is one of the most important things to establish in students' schoolwork, and extremely beneficial to them in every area of life. Charlotte Mason often likened habits to train tracks that allow a child's life to run smoothly and evenly through the day. Her thoughts on this apply to both home life and school life:

> *"The mother who takes pains to endow her children with good habits secures for herself smooth and easy days; While she who lets their habits take care of themselves has a weary life of endless friction with the children."*
> ~ Charlotte Mason, *Home Education*, p. 136

Young children thrive when they know what to expect next; the daily routine or order of schoolwork creates an environment that optimizes learning.

An important habit for children to devlop is the that of paying careful attention to what they are doing. Short lessons at this age makes this habit much easier for all children to learn. Consider moving to a different kind of activity between each section of the daily lessons. For example, just after completing copybook, have students do some kind of physical motion—even if it is just getting up and stretching or sharpening their pencils. Particularly after any part of the lesson that requires strong concentration and close eye focus, try to incorporate a short physical activity.

ℭ Sample Lesson Plan

Here is a suggested order for completing the daily work in *Language Lessons for Children Primers.*

1. Begin each day's session with students by reading the weekly selection aloud. Make sure you read with proper pauses and with feeling and expression. On the first day of a new lesson, talk with students about the copybook selection and make sure they understand it. On subsequent days, continue to read the copybook selection aloud to students, and then have them read it to you. Set a goal to have the students read with good feeling and expression by the end of the week. Encourage students to memorize the copybook selection. Each week's selection has a drawing page opposite. Have students illustrate the copybook selection on this page at some point during the week.

2. Have students write the date in the "Today is..." section. As they are learning how to do this, write the date out for them to copy. Use this format:

Monday, October 3, 2014

3. Go over the day's copybook selection with students as detailed in Pedagogy and Practice above. At first, students may need you to sit with them as they complete their work. Do this as long as necessary, but work towards more independence in completing lessons over time. Copybook sessions should be short (five to ten minutes). If necessary, complete this over several copybook sessions in one day. Have students check their work at the end of each session.

4. Help students complete the spelling or grammar lesson accurately.

5. Do the reading and narration, picture study, or nature study lesson.

It is worth repeating: keep lessons short and varied. Avoid having young children complete all of this work in one long sitting. Here is an example of how I might structure Day 2 for my eight-year-old son at home.

* Read weekly selection together.
* Complete about half of the copybook selection and check it.
* Feed the cat.
* Review the spelling or grammar lesson; complete and check.
* Go over the vocabulary for the narration lesson.
* Get up and do a little bit of stretching or run around the outside of the house three times.
* Move to the sofa to do the reading and narration lesson.
* Enjoy a snack.
* Complete the rest of the copybook selection and check it.

Of course, your particulars will vary. Some students will be able to sit and focus for longer periods of time, but I have found that most students, particularly boys, do best with this kind of routine.

Optional Enrichment Ideas

CR **Memorize the Weekly Selection** Try to schedule a recitation before an audience periodically. Parents, grandparents, siblings, and friends generally make an encouraging audience, as do residents of a local elder care facility. Recitation is wonderful preparation for public speaking.

CR **Read the Whole Book** If the copybook selection comes from a longer book or story, try to read the entire story at some point during the week.

CR **Read More Books** Find books on your shelf or at the library that give more information on the nature topic for the week. Look for books with lots of pictures and illustrations. Also check the *1000 Good Books* list, which suggests books for read alouds for every age group:

www.classical-homeschooling.org/celoop/1000.html

CR **Plan a Field Trip** to a local art gallery, zoo, arboretum, nature preserve, or observatory.

A Note to Home Educating Parents[1]

"Richer than I you can never be-
I had a Mother who read to me."
~ Strickland Gillilan

Read, read, read to your child! I cannot emphasize this strongly enough. Take it from a mom of grown children—this is a fleeting opportunity, so treasure the time reading with your child. And keep reading to your child even as he reaches the teen and young adult years. The ideas, characters, and language in the books you read together will become part of the 'language' of your family, and give you countless opportunities for discussion.

Do not allow busy schedules to crowd out this vital component of developing the soul of your child. Prioritize reading with your child above co-ops, enrichment classes, and even sports. It is one of the best investments you can make in your child's education, as well as in your relationship with him. Make reading aloud a routine in your homeschool and in your daily life with your child. Guard this time with your life.

Select worthy books with lovely illustrations. Choose books both you and your child will enjoy, and do not forget to reread favorites. There are so many marvelous classic children's books. Do not waste time reading 'twaddle'—books that are shallow and condescending to children, as unfortunately many children's books are. Be discerning in your choices. Just as setting healthy eating patterns early

---

1 This note is excerpted from a talk entitled Joy in the Homeschool Journey which I have given to several local homeschool groups.

in life can create lifelong healthy habits, so establishing a taste for worthy books in his early years can help train his appetite for great books in later years.

Horace E. Scudder, the late nineteenth century editor of The Atlantic Monthly and compiler of great literature for children wrote, "There is no academy on earth equal to a mother's reading to her child." I could not agree more.

PRIMER ONE AUTUMN
TEACHING NOTES & HELPS

SOLOMON GRUNDY

Solomon Grundy,
Born on Monday,
Christened on Tuesday,
Married on Wednesday,
Took ill on Thursday,
Worse on Friday,
Died on Saturday,
Buried on Sunday:
This is the end
Of Solomon Grundy

~ Traditional English Nursery Rhyme

ℭℛ COPYBOOK & DICTATION

Review the instructions for Copybook and for Dication in the Pedagogy & Practice section of the Introduction.

Note that the first letter of each line of poetry is capitalized.

ℭℛ SPELLING, GRAMMAR, AND WORD USAGE

Review the instructions for Spelling, Grammar, and Word Usage in the Pedagogy & Practice section of the Introduction.

The concept of "think to spell" is a way for students to learn correct spelling of words with unusual letter combinations or silent letters like the days of the week or the months of the year. Pronounce the word the way it is spelled, emphasizing the silent or unusual letters within the word. Use this method with *Tuesday* (*Tu · ES · day*) and *Wednesday* (*Wed · NES · day*). "Think to spell" will not always correspond to proper syllabication, as in the word *Tuesday*, which the dictionary divides *Tues · day*. When proper syllabication is needed, the dictionary is the final authority.

○ঽ NATURE STUDY

Review the instructions for Nature Study in the Pedagogy & Practice section of the Introduction.

Finding Direction Even in this age of Google Maps and GPS devices, a good sense of direction is a basic skill everyone needs to develop. It is really a safety precaution, particularly valuable when young people begin to drive.

Begin by helping students to understand direction in the context of their immediate surroundings. If students do not have a compass at home, they could use the "old-fashioned" method—look toward the rising sun. For most of the United States, they will be looking eastward. This is just a general idea, and may not be 100% accurate, but it will yield a general orientation. Figure out the other directions using the mnemonic **Never Eat Shredded Wheat.**

The *Primer Resources Webpage* contains links to sites that are helpful for learning to find direction with and without a compass. Look for enrichment activities there also.

AUTUMN, WEEK 2

from THE TALE OF SQUIRREL NUTKIN

One autumn when the nuts were ripe, and the leaves on the hazel bushes were golden and green—Nutkin and Twinkleberry and all the other little squirrels came out of the wood, and down to the edge of the lake.

They made little rafts out of twigs, and they paddled away over the water to Owl Island to gather nuts.

Each squirrel had a little sack and a large oar, and spread out his tail for a sail.

~ Beatrix Potter

൧ COPYBOOK & DICTATION

Note that the first word of each paragraph of prose is indented. In typeset, you will sometimes see paragraphs that are not indented when they are separated by a line, as in this book. Show this to students, but always have them indent when they are writing by hand.

൧ SPELLING, GRAMMAR, AND WORD USAGE

Day 1 *Making Plurals* Note that this discussion of making words plural refers only to words that name persons, places, things, or ideas (nouns). Nouns, along with other parts of speech, will be introduced in *Primer Two*.

To help students determine which words use **-es** when making plurals, have them listen to the end of the root word. If it ends in /ch/, /sh/, /x/, /s/, and /z/, it will probably require an **-es.** Tell your students that if the root word *hisses*, they should add **-es.**

Note that not all words ending in **-f** change to a **-v-** when adding **-es.** Instruct students to say the plural word, and see whether if the **-f** makes a **v** sound. The words with no change continue to say the **f** sound in their plural forms. Tell students they will need to listen carefully to proper pronunciation in order to spell correctly.

Answers: nuts, wishes, loaves, woods, sashes, sheaves, lakes, marshes, knives

Day 2 *Making Past Tense* To help students understand the concept of past tense, draw on their natural language abilities by using the words *today* and *yesterday* to give context. Have them say "Today, I..." and add the word in its correct present form. Then have them say "Yesterday, I..." and add word in its correct past form. For example: "Today I gather. Yesterday, I gathered."

Answers: gathered, landed, came, called, planted, had, rowed, lifted, was, filled, picked, told

Day 3 *Rhyming Words* Have students replace the beginning consonant(s) with different single letter and letter blends. A list of beginning blends is included in the Appendix of *Teaching Helps* for handy reference. Be sure you help students spell the rhyming words correctly, since they may differ from the spelling pattern of the original. If you need help, use a rhyming dictionary or online rhyming resource.

Answers (will vary): whale, nail, sale, bail, bale, gale, fail, veil

Day 4 *Making Past Tense & Plural*
Past Tense: got, sang, hunted, pulled, made, took

Plural: bushes, leaves, oars

ℭℜ NATURE STUDY
Finding Direction See Week 1 Nature Study Teaching Notes.

Autumn, Week 3

from Just a Happy Day

"After all," Anne had said to Marilla once, "I believe the nicest and sweetest days are not those on which anything very splendid or wonderful or exciting happens but just those that bring simple little pleasures, following one another softly, like pearls slipping off a string."

Life at Green Gables was full of just such days, for Anne's adventures and misadventures, like those of other people, did not all happen at once, but were sprinkled over the year, with long stretches of harmless, happy days between, filled with work and dreams and laughter and lessons. Such a day came late in August. In the forenoon Anne and Diana rowed the delighted twins down the pond to the sandshore to pick "sweet grass" and paddle in the surf, over which the wind was harping an old lyric learned when the world was young.

~ *Anne of Avonlea*, by Lucy Maude Montgomery

Copybook & Dictation

This is our first copywork selection with quotations. Make sure students carefully observe where the punctuation and capitalization are placed.

Spelling, Grammar, and Word Usage

Day 1 *Making Past Tense & Plurals*
Past Tense: were, brought, followed, did, came, learned

Plural: pearls, stretches, lyrics

Day 2 *Rhyming Words*
Answers: (rhyming answers may vary) lurk, shirk, clerk, jerk, quirk; plays, rays, raise, weighs, craze, blaze, gaze

30

Day 3 *Phonogram -or after w*
Answers: worlds, works, words, worms, fireworks, silkworms

Day 4 *Days of the Week & Abbreviations* Teach the simplest form of abbreviation for the days of the week (first three letters followed by a period). You may wish to point out that there are other ways to abbreviate. Sometimes Tuesday and Thursday will use four or five letters followed by a period (Tues., Thurs.) Days of the week can also be abbreviated with just one or two capital letters and no period (M, TU, W, TH, F, SA, SU).

Answers: Mon., Tue., Wed., Thu., Fri., Sat., Sun.

℘ NATURE STUDY
Finding Direction See Week 1 Nature Study Teaching Notes.

AUTUMN, WEEK 4

JESUS, TENDER SHEPHERD

Jesus, tender Shepherd, hear me;
Bless Thy little lamb tonight:
Through the darkness be Thou near me,
Keep me safe till morning light.

All this day Thy hand has led me,
And I thank Thee for Thy care;
Thou has warmed me, clothed, and fed me;
Listen to my evening prayer.

Let my sins be all forgiven;
Bless the friends I love so well:
Take us all at last to heaven,

Happy there with Thee to dwell. Amen..

~ Mary Duncan

☙ COPYBOOK & DICTATION
See *Names Referring to the Trinity* in the Copybook section of Pedagogy and Practice.

Explain to students that *till* is short for *until*. It is a frequently used convention in poetry to shorten words, leaving out letters or replacing them with an apostrophe, in order to create or to keep a certain meter. The technical term for this is *elision*. Help students look for other examples of this in a poetry book.

This poem has been set to music as a hymn with at least two different tunes. If time permits, find and listen to them online.

☙ SPELLING, GRAMMAR, AND WORD USAGE
Day 2 *Words with Silent Letters* refer back to Week 1 notes on "think to spell" as needed.

Day 4 *Making Past Tense & Plurals*
Past Tense: heard, thanked, listened, took, hastened, kept

Plural: hands, churches, elves

☙ NATURE STUDY
Finding Direction See Week 1 Nature Study Teaching Notes.

Autumn, Week 5

from Eeyore Loses a Tail and Pooh Finds One

So Winnie-the-Pooh went off to find Eeyore's tail.

It was a fine spring morning in the forest as he started out. Little soft clouds played happily in a blue sky, skipping from time to time in front of the sun as if they had come to put it out, and then sliding away suddenly so that the next might have his turn. Through them and between them the sun shone bravely; and a copse which had worn its firs all the year round seemed old and dowdy now beside the new green lace which the beeches had put on so prettily.

~ *Winnie-the-Pooh*, by A. A. Milne

℃ Spelling, Grammar, and Word Usage

Note the rule for adding suffixes on Day 2 only applies consistently to one-syllable words and only when the suffix begins with a vowel. Help students identify the two sounds you hear in the consonant **x** (**k** + **s**). Also, point out that **y** and **w** are not doubled if they are used as part of a vowel digraph, as in *monkey*, *stay*, *toy*, *snow*, *saw*, and *new* since you hear only one sound. Refer back to your phonics or spelling program if you need additional help in reviewing this concept.

Day 1 *Rhyming Words*
Answers (will vary): shout, pout, trout, doubt, drought

Day 2 *Adding Suffixes*
Answers: skipping, getting, playing, putting, sinning, boxing, shipping, begging, blowing

Day 3 *Adding Suffixes*

33

Answers: skipped, begged, played, shipped, bagged, boxed, sinned, stopped, rowed

Day 4 *Making Plurals*
Answers: tails, springs, mornings, clouds, greens, beeches, grasses, matches, hooves

℞ NATURE STUDY
Finding Direction See Week 1 Nature Study Teaching Notes.

AUTUMN, WEEK 6

AUTUMN

The morns are meeker than they were,
The nuts are getting brown;
The berry's cheek is plumper,
The rose is out of town.

The maple wears a gayer scarf,
The field a scarlet gown.
Lest I should be old fashioned,
I'll put a trinket on.

~ Emily Dickinson

℞ COPYBOOK & DICTATION
Students may notice and mention, as mine frequently do, that *gown* and *on* do not exactly rhyme. Explain that this is called a **slant rhyme**—the final consonant sounds match, but not necessarily the vowel sound of the final syllable. Emily Dickinson's poetry abounds with slant rhymes.

ℭ Spelling, Grammar, and Word Usage

See Week 5 notes on adding a suffix beginning with a vowel to a one-syllable word.

Day 2 *Adding Suffixes*

Answers: skipper, zipper, gayer, shipper, bigger, boxer, sinner, stopper, rower, flipper, meeker, plumper

Day 4 *Rhyming Words*

Answers (will vary): brown, crown, clown, noun; her, blur, fir, myrrh, stir, purr; hose, blows, clothes, close, shows, throws

ℭ Nature Study

Tree Leaf Identification Students should learn to identify the most common trees found in your geographical location. Leaf identification is a good place to start.

Select trees near your home or school, and have students collect one or more leaves from the tree. Try to get intact leaves. If possible, collect the seed of the tree. Some common seed types include cones, acorns, or helicopters. If the tree is in an area where you are not allowed to remove leaves and seeds, make careful notes and drawings to aid you in identification. Another possibility is to take digital photos for this step.

Observe the tree. Do a quick sketch the shape of the whole tree in your nature notebook. Look at how the leaves are arranged on each stem, and make sketches. Is there only one leaf on a stem, or are there multiple leaves on the stem? If there are multiple leaves, look carefully at how the leaves are arranged on the stem. Are they directly across from each other (opposite) or do they alternate along the stem? Help students sketch and make notes as they observe.

Observe the leaf. Is it a broad leaf or a needle? What color is it? How is it shaped? Does it have a jagged, tooth-shaped edge or a smooth edge? What do the veins look like?

Bring the leaf back home and have students carefully draw it on the page provided in their *Primer* books. They should take their time and include the details you have discussed.

Using what you have collected, see if you can identify the type of tree using the links to identification keys.

Optional Enrichment Activities See the *Primer Resources Webpage* for links to instructions.

* Choose a tree near your house and make a sketch of it each month to observe how it changes through the year.
* Press leaves between two sheets of wax paper to preserve them.
* Do leaf rubbings.

AUTUMN, WEEK 7

from THE JUBILATE DEO

Make a joyful shout to the Lord, all you lands!
Serve the Lord with gladness;
Come before His presence with singing.
Know that the Lord, He is God;
It is He who has made us, and not we ourselves;

We are His people and the sheep of His pasture.

Enter into His gates with thanksgiving,

And into His courts with praise.

Be thankful to Him, and bless His name.

~ Psalm 100:1-4, New King James Version

℞ COPYBOOK & DICTATION

See *A Note About Scripture Copybook Selections* and *A Note About Names Referring to the Trinity* in the Copybook section of Pedagogy and Practice.

Jubilate Deo is the Latin name for this Psalm found in the Anglican *Book of Common Prayer*, among other places. The only substantive change to these verses from the King James version is the word *shout* is substituted for the word *noise* in the first line. If students have memorized this in the King James Version already, you may prefer to have them copy it with *noise*.

℞ SPELLING, GRAMMAR, AND WORD USAGE

Day 1 *Making Compounds with "Full"* This rule also applies to all (all + ways = always; all + ready = already, all + together = altogether). You may wish to show students these words also.

Answers: joyful, thankful, hopeful, restful, helpful, peaceful, graceful

Day 2 *Making Plurals*

Answers: people or peoples (depending on usage, either may be correct), sheep, selves, courts, lands, shouts, we, names, pastures, calves, foxes, deer

37

Day 3 *Adding Suffixes to Words Ending with a Silent e*
Answers: making, serving, praising, giving, naming, pasturing, loving, pleasing, paddling

Day 4 *Rhyming Words*
Answers (will vary): show, mow, go, though, toe, woe, whoa; ringing, bringing, swinging, springing

ᙣ NATURE STUDY
Tree Leaf Identification See Week 6 Nature Study Teaching Notes.

AUTUMN, WEEK 8

from LAND

At daybreak one cold November morning, a glad shout rang through the ship. "Land! Land!"

Yes, there lay the land—that new land which was to be their home and ours.

There were no rocky cliffs like those of England. Before them rose tall, green pine trees, and great oaks still wearing their dress of reddish brown.

Not a town or a single house could they see. No smoke rose from the forest to tell them where a village lay hidden. Not a sound was heard but the whistling of the cold wind through the ropes and masts, and the lapping of the water about the boat.

~ *Stories of the Pilgrims,* by Margaret Pumphrey

ᙣ SPELLING, GRAMMAR, AND WORD USAGE
Day 2 *Adding Suffixes*
Answers: redder, reddest, reddish, madder, maddest,

madly, lapped, lapping, lapful

Day 3 *Adding Suffixes*
Answers: smoking, whistling, hiding; smoked, whistled, forced

Day 4 *Adding Suffixes*
Answers: planner, planning, landing, singer, hidden, whistler, nicer, smoky, windy

CR NATURE STUDY
Tree Leaf Identification See Week 6 Nature Study Teaching Notes

AUTUMN, WEEK 9

from ALL PEOPLE THAT ON EARTH DO DWELL

All people that on earth do dwell,
Sing to the Lord with cheerful voice;
Him serve with fear, His praise forthtell,
Come ye before Him and rejoice.

The Lord, ye know, is God indeed;
Without our aid He did us make;
We are his folk, He doth us feed,
And for His sheep He doth us take.

~ William Kethe, 1561 (based on Psalm 100)

CR COPYBOOK & DICTATION
See *A Note About Names Referring to the Trinity* in the Copybook section of Pedagogy and Practice.

Have students compare this hymn, which is based on Psalm

100, with the Bible passage from Week 8.

❧ Spelling, Grammar, and Word Usage
Day 1 *Phonogram* oi English words do not end in -i, because the $/\bar{\imath}/$ sound is usually spelled with y at the end of a word, but there are a few exceptions. Foreign words like *ski* (Norwegian) have been adopted into our language and have retained the final -i. And of course, the pronoun **I** ends with i. Tell students to remember, "I am unique!"

Day 2 *Making Past Tense*
Answers: did, sang, praised, was, came, rejoiced, fed, were, took

Day 4 *Rhyming Words*
Answers (will vary): sell, well, fell, swell, quell; bead, read, seed, creed, breed

❧ Nature Study
Mammals Mammals for student observation should not be too difficult to find. Subjects might include the pets in your own home, friendly squirrels and chipmunks in your yard, farm animals, or animals at the zoo. Siblings and fellow students are mammals too.

Begin in Week 9 by explaining and discussing the characteristics of mammals. See if students can name an animal besides a mammal that also has each listed characteristic.

✓ *Mammals have a backbone.* Show students how to locate their own backbones. Explain how the backbone gives structure to the whole body. Find a picture of a human or animal skeleton and point out the backbone. Tell students that the backbone, also called the spine, is actually made up of many bones called **vertebrae** (singular **vertebra**). Animals with backbones are called **vertebrates**. Besides mammals, a few other vertebrates are fish, reptiles, and birds.

✓ *Mammals are warm-blooded.* This means the animal's body temperature remains constant, as opposed to a cold-blooded animal whose body temperature is determined by its environment. Birds are warm-blooded. Snakes, reptiles, insects, and fish are cold-blooded.

✓ *Mammals have lungs and breathe air.* Mammals breathe in oxygen and give off carbon dioxide. Other animals with lungs include birds, amphibians, and reptiles. Fish do not have lungs, but they have gills to take in oxygen from the water.

✓ *Mammals have skin with hair on it.* Some animals have a lot of hair or fur, such as the bear, and some have very little hair in comparison, like a human. Do birds have hair? How about fish or reptiles?

✓ *Most mammals give birth to live young.* A few mammals, like the platypus, do lay eggs instead of giving birth to live young, but this is a rare exception. Birds, fish, insects, and most reptiles lay eggs; there are a few reptiles that give birth to live young.

✓ *Mammals feed their young with milk.* All mammals have

mammary glands which produce milk to feed their young—hence, the name *mammal*. Birds bring worms and berries to their young; insects lay their eggs where their young can find food when they hatch.

Help students think of ten mammals. Ask students to start in their own homes or yards by naming pets that might be mammals. Next ask them to name some farm animals. Then ask them to name wild animals in the meadows or woodlands (or prairie or desert or jungle) of your area. Finally, ask students to name some more exotic animals they have seen at the zoo or read about in books. If you are not sure whether a particular animal is a mammal, an internet search or a field guide should help you figure it out. There are many, many animals, but here is a short list in case you get stuck: dog, cat, horse, cow, sheep, goat, pig, lion, tiger, bear, monkey, squirrel, mouse, chipmunk, fox, beaver, rabbit, skunk, groundhog, opossum, deer, and human.

Students will choose one mammal each week to observe, discuss, and draw. Talk with students and choose which mammals they would like to study. Co-op teachers may assign different mammals to each student and ask them to give a short presentation in the next class.

If you do not have immediate access to mammals for observation, check out library books or find online resources to view and learn about specific mammals. Check the *Primer Resources Webpage* for links.

The goal of these lessons is for your students to simply observe a mammal and talk about it with you. Do not worry if they cannot talk about every point listed in their Primers.

42

Just ask them to keep observing through the week, and perhaps read a little about the mammal they have chosen.

Since wild animals tend to be shy of humans, and may be dangerous, students will probably need to use a picture to do their drawings for non-domesticated mammals. See links on the *Primer Resources Webpage*.

AUTUMN, WEEK 10

from ALL PEOPLE THAT ON EARTH DO DWELL

O enter then His courts with praise,
Approach with joy His courts unto;
Praise, laud, and bless His name always,
For it is seemly so to do.

For why? The Lord our God is good,
His mercy is forever sure;
His truth at all times stood,
And shall from age to age endure.

~ William Kethe, 1561 (based on Psalm 100)

℞ COPYBOOK & DICTATION
See *A Note About Names Referring to the Trinity* in the Copybook section of Pedagogy and Practice.

Again, have students compare this hymn, based on Psalm 100, with the Bible passage from Week 8.

ℭℛ Spelling, Grammar, and Word Usage

Day 1 Adding Suffixes

Answers: praising, blessed, surely, aging, doing, surer, littler, muddy, mighty

Day 4 Rhyming Words

Answers (will vary): who, grew, due, moo, you, blue, chew; stood, would, could, should, hood

ℭℛ Nature Study

Mammals See Week 9 Nature Study Teaching Notes.

Autumn, Week 11

from The Gospel of Luke

Then the angel said to them, "Do not be afraid, for behold, I bring you good tidings of great joy which will be to all people. For there is born to you this day in the city of David a Savior, who is Christ the Lord. And this will be the sign to you: You will find a Babe wrapped in swaddling cloths, lying in a manger."

And suddenly there was with the angel a multitude of the heavenly host praising God and saying:

"Glory to God in the highest,
And on earth peace, goodwill toward men!"

~ Luke 2:10-14, New King James Version

ℭℛ Copybook & Dictation

See *A Note About Scripture Copybook Selections* and *A Note About Names Referring to the Trinity* in the Copybook section of Pedagogy and Practice.

Point out the punctuation carefully in this copywork selection, especially the quotations.

○ Spelling, Grammar, and Word Usagee

Day 1 *Homonyms* Learning to spell and use homonyms correctly will help students avoid many common spelling errors. Whenever students write homonyms, have them use each one in a sentence orally so you can make sure they know which spelling to use in context.

Answers: here; sale; rowed, road; one; male; four, fore; week

Day 2 *Adding Suffixes*
Answers: wrapped, wrapping, swaddling, singing, beings, highest, saying, peaceful, shiny, praising, clapped, suddenly

Day 3 *Making Past Tense*
Answers: said, praised, brought, was, found, swaddled, went, told, sang

○ Nature Study
Mammals See Week 9 Nature Study Teaching Notes.

Autumn, Week 12
_____

Away in a Manger

Away in a manger, no crib for a bed,
The little Lord Jesus lay down His sweet head;
The stars in the bright sky looked down where He lay,
The little Lord Jesus, asleep on the hay.

The cattle are lowing, the baby awakes,
But little Lord Jesus no crying He makes;
I love thee, Lord Jesus! Look down from the sky,
And stay by my cradle till morning is nigh.

Be near me, Lord Jesus, I ask Thee to stay
Close by me forever, and love me, I pray;
Bless all the dear children in Thy tender care,
And fit us for heaven, to live with Thee there..

~ Traditional Christmas Carol

ℭℜ SPELLING, GRAMMAR, AND WORD USAGE
Day 1 *Making Past Tense*
Answers: looked, slept, lowed, made, loved, awoke, stayed, prayed, lived

Day 2 *Rhyming Words*
Answers (will vary): bay, stay, they, prey, sleigh, stray; sigh, my, die, buy, shy, spry; led, lead, shred, spread, read

Day 2 *Homonyms*
Answer: deer

ℭℜ NATURE STUDY
Mammals See Week 9 Nature Study Teaching Notes.

PRIMER ONE WINTER
TEACHING NOTES & HELPS

WINTER, WEEK 1

from A CALENDAR

January brings the snow,
Makes our feet and fingers glow.

February brings the rain,
Thaws the frozen lake again.

March brings breezes, loud and shrill,
To stir the dancing daffodil.

April brings the primrose sweet,
Scatters daisies at our feet.

May brings flocks of pretty lambs
Skipping by their fleecy dams.

June brings tulips, lilies, roses,
Fills the children's hands with posies.

~ Sara Coleridge

℞ COPYBOOK & DICTATION

Review the instructions for Copybook and for Dication in the Pedagogy & Practice section of the Introduction.

℞ SPELLING, GRAMMAR, AND WORD USAGE

Review the instructions for *Spelling, Grammar, and Word Usage* in the Pedagogy & Practice section of the Introduction.

Day 1 *Months of the Year* Review the concept of "think to spell" in the Teaching Notes for Autumn Week 1. This is a handy way to help students learn correct spelling of words with unusual letter combinations or silent letters. Pronounce the word the way it is spelled, emphasizing the silent or unusual letters within the word.

Work with students each day to memorize the months of the year in order.

CR NATURE STUDY[1]

> *"The heavens declare the glory*
> *of God..." ~ Psalm 19:1*

Review the instructions for Nature Study in the Pedagogy & Practice section of the Introduction.

The Night Sky Before you read this introduction to students, write the bolded words on the board.

> **Astronomy,** the study of the heavens, is said to be the most ancient of the sciences. References to the heavens—the sun, the moon, and the stars— are plentiful in literature, legends, folklore, and especially in Scripture. Psalm 19:1 tells us, "The heavens declare the glory of God..." These nature study lessons are designed to introduce you the glories of the night sky as you begin to make your own observations about them.

> The moon's appearance changes every night, going from a tiny crescent sliver to a big round circle (**Full Moon**), then back to a sliver before it disappears for a night or two (**New Moon**). The changes in the shape of the moon that we see

1 All information about constellations in the Primer series is from the perspective of North America. If you live in a different location, you will need to adjust. See the Primer Resources Webpage for online resources.

through the 28 day **lunar cycle** are called **phases**. Check the *Primer Resources Webpage* for links to websites where the monthly **lunar phases** are illustrated.

We say that the moon is **waxing** as it goes from a **New Moon** to a **Full Moon,** and we say it is **waning** as it moves from a **Full Moon** back to a **New Moon**. In both of these periods, we see a **crescent** shape and a **gibbous** shape. The word gibbous comes from Latin word *gibbus*, meaning *hump*.

You can tell whether the moon is waxing or waning by looking at the **horns** or points of the crescent. When the horns point to the left, the moon is **waxing**. When the horns point to the right, the moon is **waning**.

Did you know that each month's moon has a name? You have probably heard of the **Harvest Moon,** which is in September or October. How do you suppose it got its name? (*It occurs during the time when farmers are harvesting their crops. Farmers are able to work in their fields by the light of the moon far into the night for several days around the time of the full moon.*)

Native Americans had names for each moon of the year. The *Farmer's Almanac* lists some of these (see *Primer Resources Webpage* for link).

Students are instructed to keep a calendar of the phases of the moon for one month. The winter months are a good time

to do this with the earlier time of nightfall and moonrise. A calendar with blanks large enough to draw and label the phases of the moon through the month is provided in the Appendix of *Primer One Winter*.

Students could also make a copy of the calendar onto cardstock and post it on a bulletin board or the refrigerator at home where it will serve as a reminder to observe and record.

WINTER, WEEK 2

from A CALENDAR

Hot July brings cooling showers,
Apricots and gillyflowers.

August brings the sheaves of corn,
Then the harvest home is borne.

Warm September brings the fruit;
Sportsmen then begin to shoot.

Fresh October brings the pheasant;
Then to gather nuts is pleasant.

Dull November brings the blast;
Then the leaves are whirling fast.

Chill December brings the sleet,
Blazing fire, and Christmas treat.

~ Sara Coleridge

℞ SPELLING, GRAMMAR, AND WORD USAGE
Continue working with students each day to memorize

the months in order. Show them how each month has a corresponding number which may be used in writing the date instead of the month name. For example,

January 5, 2014 may also be written **1/5/14.**

○Ꝛ NATURE STUDY
The Constellations Before you read this introduction to students, write the bolded words on the board.

> When you look up at the sky on a clear night, what do you see? Hundreds, thousands, even millions of stars twinkling in inky darkness. Truly, "the heavens declare the glory of God." (Psalm 19)
>
> Think about this: the stars you see in the night sky are the same stars that shone over Nazareth when Jesus was a boy. They are the same stars that delighted and intrigued the ancient Greeks, and that helped guide Columbus and his men to America.
>
> From the beginning of recorded history, men have noticed groupings of stars that seemed to make pictures in the sky. These star groupings are called **constellations**, and most of them are still known by the names that the ancient Greeks gave to them.
>
> If you live away from the lights of a city or town, on a clear night you can see The **Milky Way**, a hazy ribbon that looks almost like dust stretching

across the sky. What you are seeing is one of the spiral arms of our own galaxy of stars. The ancient Greeks said that the Milky Way was the pathway to the throne room of the gods on Mount Olympus.

It is fun to learn the name of constellations and to be able to recognize them in the night sky. Over the next few weeks, we will learn some of the most familiar.

If you need help in finding the position of the constellations where you live, check the *Primer Resources Webpage* for a free interactive sky map where you can put in the name of the city nearest you.

Optional Enrichment Read the stories that the ancient Greeks made up to explain the the star patterns. See the *Primer Resources Webpage*.

WINTER, WEEK 3

from PIGLET MEETS A HEFFALUMP

The Sun was still in bed, but there was a lightness in the sky over the Hundred Acre Wood which seemed to show that it was waking up and would soon be kicking off the clothes. In the half-light, the Pine Trees looked cold and lonely, and the Very Deep Pit seemed deeper than it was, and Pooh's jar of honey at the bottom was something mysterious, a shape and no more. But as he got nearer to it his nose told him that it was indeed honey, and his tongue came out and began to polish up his mouth.

"Bother!" said Pooh, as he got his nose inside the jar. "A Heffalump has been eating it!" And then he thought a little and said, "Oh no, I did. I forgot."

Indeed, he had eaten most of it. But there was a little left at the very bottom of the jar, and he pushed his head right in and began to lick.

~ *Winnie-the-Pooh*, by A.A. Milne

ℭ COPYBOOK & DICTATION

A. A. Milne uses capitalization to show **personification** of the places, trees, and objects in Christopher Robin's world. He is giving qualities or characteristics of persons to the *Sun*, the *Pine Trees*, and even to the *Very Deep Pit*. Christopher Robin speaks of the Forest and Outland as proper place names because to him there is only ONE Forest and only ONE Outland. Personification will be discussed at length in future books. For now, if students do not ask questions about A. A. Milne's use of capitals, let it pass.

Note that the first word of each paragraph of prose is indented. In typeset, you will sometimes see paragraphs that are not indented when they are separated by a line, as in this book. Show this to students, but always have them indent when they are writing by hand.

ℭ SPELLING, GRAMMAR, AND WORD USAGE

Days 1 and 2 *Writing Names* Help students as needed by writing names, places, and holidays on the whiteboard or a piece of paper for them to copy.

Day 1 *Writing Names*
Answers (examples): John Paul Jones; Louisville

Day 2 *Writing Dates*
Answers (examples): I was born on June 5, 2000; My father was born September 1, 1960.

Day 3 *Writing Names with Titles*
Answers (examples): Mr. Snagsby, Mrs. Smallweed, Rev. Chadband, Aunt Esther, Cousin Ada, Dr. Woodcourt

Day 4 *Months of the Year*
Answers: 1. January 2. February 3. March 4. April 5. May 6. June 7. July 8. August 9. September 10. October 11. November 12. December

ᙡ Nature Study
Ursa Major and the Big Dipper Before you read this introduction to students, write the bolded words on the board.

The **Big Dipper** is one of the most familiar star groupings, although it is not technically a constellation in its own right but is part of a larger constellation called **Ursa Major** (the Big Bear). Star groupings like this within a constellation are called **asterisms**. Because many of the stars in Ursa Major are faint, it is hard to see the entire constellation in the night sky. But everyone can see The Big Dipper, the asterism made by the seven brightest stars in Ursa Major. See the *Primer Resources Webpage* for a link to see this asterism.

WINTER, WEEK 4

from PSALM 19

The heavens declare the glory of God;
    and the firmament shows His handiwork.
Day unto day utters speech,
    and night unto night reveals knowledge.
There is no speech nor language
    where their voice is not heard.
Their line has gone out through all the earth,
    and their words to the end of the world.

~ Psalm 19:1-5, New King James Version

ଓ COPYBOOK & DICTATION

See *A Note About Scripture Copybook Selections* and *A Note About Names Referring to the Trinity* in the Copybook section of Pedagogy and Practice.

ଓ SPELLING, GRAMMAR, AND WORD USAGE

Day 1 *Phonogram* **dge** Discuss why the silent final **-e** is needed in this phonogram: Usually **g** says **/j/** before **e, i,** or **y.** (Note that there are some words that make the hard **/g/** sound before **e, i,** or **y,** for example, in 'get' or 'give'.) Before any other letter, or at the end of a word, **g** always makes the hard **/g/** sound. Ask students why the silent final **-e** is retained in the compound word 'sledgehammer' *(in order to keep the g soft)*.

Day 2 *Writing Sentences*
Answers (examples): Valentine's Day is February 14. Uncle Charlie always makes me laugh. My Sunday School teacher

is Mrs. Collins.

Day 4 *The Months of the Year*
Answers: 1. Jan. 2. Feb. 3. Mar. 4. Apr. 5. May
6. Jun. 7. Jul. 8. Aug. 9. Sep. 10. Oct. 11. Nov.
12. Dec.

℘ NATURE STUDY

The Little Dipper and Polaris Before you read this introduction to students, find the link to a picture of the Little Dipper on the *Primer Resources Webpage*, and write the bolded words on the board.

Notice how the *bowl* of the **Big Dipper** points in a staight line toward the **North Star**, or **Polaris**. Polaris is the brightest star in the **Little Dipper**, the familiar asterism in the constellation of **Ursa Minor** (the Little Bear).

Polaris is a very important star, because it is a *fixed* star, always directly above the horizon at due north. The other stars appear to rotate around it. Because of this, Polaris can always be used for finding direction at night.

WINTER, WEEK 5

THE MOON

The moon has a face like the clock in the hall;
She shines on thieves on the garden wall,
On streets and fields and harbour quays,
And birdies asleep in the forks of the trees.

The squalling cat and the squeaking mouse,
The howling dog by the door of the house,
The bat that lies in bed at noon,
All love to be out by the light of the moon.

But all of the things that belong to the day
Cuddle to sleep to be out of her way;
And flowers and children close their eyes
Till up in the morning the sun shall arise.

~ Robert Louis Stevenson

Cℛ COPYBOOK & DICTATION
Quays is pronounced like *keys*, and it rhymes with *trees*.

SPELLING, GRAMMAR, AND WORD USAGE
Day 1 *Spelling Rule i before e* Ask students to identify which part of the rule each word follows. For example, ask why 'ceiling' uses **ei** (it comes after a **c**) and why 'their' uses **ei** (it says /ā/). Here are some common exceptions to this rule that should be memorized at some point by students: *either, neither, seize, leisure, weird, heifer, height, feisty, foreign, sovereign, stein, forfeit, counterfeit*. At one time, some of these were pronounced with the long **a**, but are not commonly pronounced that way now. You might arrange these words into a silly sentence or two and have students memorize them that way.

Day 2 *Writing a Friendly Letter* Instruct students to study the diagram of the standard friendly letter format in the Appendix of *Primer One Winter*. Discuss why writing letters is important, even in today's world of email and voice messages. Students might enjoy reading letters written by

58

famous people. See the *Primer Resources Webpage* for several interesting books with such letters.

Day 3 *Writing a Friendly Letter: The Greeting* The greeting of a letter is sometimes called the **salutation** . Usually, the greeting begins with 'Dear' and then the person's name followed by a comma. Instruct students to write the name they would use if they were speaking to the person face-to-face. Remind them to capitalize words that are part of a proper name.

Day 4 *Rhyming Words*
Answers (will vary): soon, spoon, June, tune, strewn; knees, seas, quays, cheese, breeze, seize, tease; pies, sighs, skies, rise, size

☯ NATURE STUDY

Cassiopeia Before you read this introduction to students, write the bolded words on the board.

> **Cassiopeia** is in the north sky. Find the **Big Dipper**, then find **Polaris**. Look on the other side of Polaris from the Big Dipper. You should see five bright stars that make a sort of sideways W in the sky. That is **Cassiopeia**.

WINTER, WEEK 6

from THE TALE OF PETER RABBIT

"Now, my dears," said Old Mrs. Rabbit one morning, "you may go into the fields or down the lane, but don't go into Mr.

McGregor's garden: your Father had an accident there; he was put in a pie by Mrs. McGregor. Now run along, and don't get into mischief. I am going out."

Then old Mrs. Rabbit took a basket and her umbrella, and went through the wood to the baker's. She bought a loaf of brown bread and five currant buns.

Flopsy, Mopsy, and Cotton-Tail, who were good little bunnies, went down the lane to gather blackberries.

But Peter, who was very naughty, ran straight away to Mr. McGregor's garden, and squeezed under the gate!

~ Beatrix Potter

℞ COPYBOOK & DICTATION

This is the first copywork selection in *Primer One Winter* with quotations. Make sure students carefully observe where the punctuation and capitalization are placed.

℞ SPELLING, GRAMMAR, AND WORD USAGE

Day 1 *Spelling Rule i before e* Again, analyze each word and have students tell you why they use **ei** or **ie**, according to the rule. See Week 5 notes on exceptions to the rules for using **ei**.

Day 2 *Writing a Friendly Letter: The Closing* If students have not yet learned cursive, consider teaching them how to write just their names in cursive. Provide neat cursive models for them to copy. The most common closing used for a friendly letter is *Love, __*. There are others you might use also. Some possibilities: *Fondly, Your friend, Sincerely, With love, Affectionately*.

Day 3 *Abbreviations* All US states with their USPS postal abbreviations are listed in the Appendix of *Primer One*

Winter.

Answers: Rd., Dr., St., Ave.

Ꮯ Nature Study

Orion and the Pleiades Before you read this introduction to students, write the bolded words on the board.

> Some of the brightest stars in the night sky are contained in the constellation **Orion** (also known as The Hunter). Look for Orion high in the sky in the winter months, although you can also see him in the spring and fall months as well. Look at the link to the constellations on the *Primer Resources Webpage.* You can see the shape of a man, with a sword and a belt. In fact, the three bright stars in **Orion's Belt** will help you to find this constellation. In the winter, the **Milky Way** passes right over Orion's head.
>
> Next to Orion is **Taurus**, The Bull. The seven bright stars in a V-shape, forming the head of the bull, are an asterism called **The Pleiades**.

Winter, Week 7

THE GOOPS

The Goops they lick their fingers,
And the Goops they lick their knives;
They spill their broth on the tablecloth—
Oh, they lead disgusting lives!

The Goops they talk while eating,
And loud and fast they chew;
And that is why I'm glad that I
Am not a Goop—are you?

~ Gellett Burgess

○ℛ COPYBOOK & DICTATION

This week, students will put together all the letter-writing lessons and write a friendly letter. Attractive stationery may help motivate and encourage students in this. There are links on the *Primer Resources Webpage* to free online printable stationery. Students may also like to illustrate their own stationery or to design it in a photo or graphics program.

○ℛ SPELLING, GRAMMAR, AND WORD USAGE

Day 4 *Rhyming Words*

Answers (will vary) knives, arrives, wives, drives, chives; moo, dew, blue, threw, stew, you, view, who; last, blast, passed, past;

○ℛ NATURE STUDY

Birds Students should learn to identify the most common birds found in your area. Begin in the backyard—installing a birdfeeder is an easy and inexpensive investment that pays huge dividends in both education and enjoyment for your whole family. Planting certain types of flowers and bushes will also attract birds.

Explain and discuss the characteristics of birds. See if students can name an animal type other than a bird that also each listed characteristic.

✓ *Birds have a backbone.* Show students their own backbone and ask if they remember its purpose (*to give structure to the whole body*). Find a picture of a bird skeleton and point out the backbone. Remind them of the technical term for an animal with a backbone: **vertebrate.** Besides birds, a few other animals which have backbones are mammals, fish, and reptiles. Point out to students that birds generally have very lightweight bones, and many bird bones are hollow. Ask students why this is so (*to make it easier for a bird to fly*).

✓ *Birds are warm-blooded.* The birds's body temperature remains constant, as opposed to a cold-blooded animal whose body temperature is determined by its environment. Mammals are also warm-blooded. Snakes, reptiles, insects, and fish are cold-blooded.

✓ *Birds have lungs and breathe air.* Many animals breathe in oxygen and give off carbon dioxide. Other animals with lungs include mammals, amphibians, and reptiles. Fish do not have lungs, but they have gills to take in oxygen from the water.

✓ *Birds have skin covered with feathers.* The feathers provide protection against cold and water. Do mammals have feathers? How about fish or reptiles?

✓ *Birds have wings.* All birds have wings and most birds use them to fly. There are a few flightless birds, however. Does any other type of animal have wings? (*Bats are mammals with wings. Insects also have wings.*)

✓ *Birds lay eggs instead of giving birth to live young.* The mother bird usually sits on the eggs to keep them warm until they hatch. Fish, insects, and most reptiles also lay eggs; although there are a few reptiles that give birth to live young. Mammals give birth to live young.

Help students think of ten types of birds. If they have trouble, an internet search or a field guide should help. There are many different types of birds, but not all of them are found in every geographic location. Here is a short list of common birds in case you get stuck: *cardinal, sparrow, bluebird, blackbird, woodpecker, owl, duck, wren, robin, hummingbird, seagull, starling, goldfinch, swallow, chicken, penguin, ostrich.*

Consider reading *The Burgess Bird Book* by Thornton Burgess with students over the next few weeks. He teaches many interesting lessons about birds and their habits in a delightful story format. It is also available as a free PDF download or a Kindle download at Gutenberg Project. Purchase or link to the download from the *Primer Resources Webpage*.

Each week, choose a bird for students to observe, discuss, and draw in Weeks 8-12. A robin is most appropriate for Week 8 to go with our literary selections. Co-op teachers may assign different birds to individual students each week, and ask students to present their observations in the next class.

Try to choose birds that come to your bird feeder if possible. If you do not have immediate access to the bird you wish to study, check out books from the library or find online resources to view and learn about it. Check the *Primer Resources Webpage* for links and resources.

The goal of these lessons is for students to simply observe a bird and talk about it with you. Do not worry if they cannot talk about every point. Just ask students to keep observing through the week, and perhaps read a little about the bird they have chosen. Since wild animals tend to be shy of humans, students will probably need a picture to do their drawing. See links on the *Primer Resources Webpage* for pictures which students can copy.

Optional Enrichment Activities (see links on the *Primer Resources Webpage* for help with these activities):

* Keep a log of birds that come to your birdfeeder.
* Study the different types of feathers birds have.
* Study different types of bird beaks.
* Learn to recognize the songs of the birds at your birdfeeder.
* Learn about what type of nests different birds build.

WINTER, WEEK 8

from INTO THE FOREST

"Do you know," said Lucy, "I really believe he means us to follow him."

"I've an idea he does," said Susan. "What do you think, Peter?"

"Well, we might as well try it," answered Peter.

The Robin appeared to understand the matter thoroughly. It kept going from tree to tree, always a few yards ahead of them, but always so near that they could easily follow it. In this way, it led them on, slightly downhill. Whenever the Robin alighted a little shower of snow would fall off the branch. Presently the clouds parted overhead and the winter sun came out and the snow all around grew dazzlingly bright.

~ *The Lion, the Witch, and the Wardrobe* by C.S. Lewis

COPYBOOK & DICTATION
Remind students to pay careful attention to the punctuation used in the quotes.

SPELLING, GRAMMAR, AND WORD USAGE
Day 1 *Could, Should, Would*
Answers: They could follow the robin. The robin would wait for them. Should they follow the robin or not?

Day 2 *Writing Contractions*
Answers: I've, he'll, she's, they're, aren't, o'clock, wouldn't, couldn't, shouldn't

Day 3 *Abbreviations*
Answers: yd., ft., mi., in.

℘ NATURE STUDY
Birds See Winter Week 7 Nature Study Teaching Notes.

WINTER, WEEK 9

THIRTY DAYS HATH SEPTEMBER

Thirty days hath September,
April, June, and November;

All the rest have thirty-one,
Excepting February alone,
Which hath but twenty-eight, in fine,
'Til leap year gives it twenty-nine.

~ Old English Rhyme

ℭℛ COPYBOOK & DICTATION

This is a wonderful poem to memorize in order to know how many days each month has. See the *Primer Resources Webpage* for a link to memory method using your knuckles.

Students may notice and mention that *alone* and *one* do not exactly rhyme. Explain that this is called a **slant rhyme.** The final consonant sounds match, but not necessarily the vowel sound of the final syllable. Look for other slant rhymes in a poetry anthology.

ℭℛ SPELLING, GRAMMAR, AND WORD USAGE

Day 2 *Commas In A Series*
Answers (examples): April, June, September, and November have thirty days. Robins, cardinals, swallows, bluebirds, and larks sing.

Day 3 *Rhyming Words*
Answers (will vary): mine, dine, sign, twine, whine, shine; moan, bone, flown, shown, thrown, stone, cyclone, unknown

NATURE STUDY
Birds See Winter Week 7 Nature Study Teaching Notes.

Winter, Week 10

The Resurrection

Very early in the morning, on the first day of the week, they came to the tomb when the sun had risen. And they said among themselves, "Who will roll away the stone from the door of the tomb for us?"

But when they looked up, they saw that the stone had been rolled away–for it was very large. And entering the tomb, they saw a young man sitting on the right side; and they were alarmed. But he said to them, "Do not be alarmed. You seek Jesus of Nazareth, who was crucified. He is risen! He is not here. See the place where they laid Him. But go and tell His disciples–and Peter–that He is going before them into Galilee; there you will see Him, as He said to you."

~ Mark 16:2-7, New King James Version

⚬ Copybook & Dictation

See *A Note About Scripture Copybook Selections* and *A Note About Names Referring to the Trinity* in the Copybook section of Pedagogy and Practice.

⚬ Spelling, Grammar, and Word Usage

Day 2 *Writing Contractions*

Answers: you're, he's, don't, where's, I'm, haven't

Day 3 *Commas In A Series*

Answers (examples): The angels told the disciples to see, go, and tell. I can see a bird feeder, two chairs, a swingset, and an oak tree outside my window.

⚬ Nature Study

Birds See Winter Week 7 Nature Study Teaching Notes.

Winter, Week 11

from Christ the Lord Is Risen Today

Christ the Lord is ris'n today; Alleluia!
Sons of men and angels say; Alleluia!
Raise your joys and triumphs high; Alleluia!
Sing, ye heav'ns, and earth, reply. Alleluia!

Vain the stone, the watch, the seal; Alleluia!
Christ hath burst the gates of hell; Alleluia!
Death in vain forbids Him rise; Alleluia!
Christ hath opened paradise. Alleluia!

~ Charles Wesley

☞ Copybook & Dictation

See *A Note About Names Referring to the Trinity* in the Copybook section of Pedagogy and Practice.

When you read this hymn with students, talk about the meaning of the word *vain* in the second stanza. Also, you might point out the word *Alleluia* is an alternate transliteration of Hebrew word *Hallelujah* which means *Praise ye the Lord*.

In the Day 1 copywork, explain to students that *heav'ns* is short for *heavens*. Refer to *Primer One Autumn* Week 4 Teaching Notes for an explanation.

☞ Spelling, Grammar, and Word Usage

Day 2 Commas In A Series
Answer (example): Birds have wings, beaks, and feathers.

Day 4 _Homonyms_

Answers: son, vane and vein, rows, hi, write and wright, too and to, aunt (depending on the dialect), hole

ੲ NATURE STUDY

Birds See Winter Week 7 Nature Study Teaching Notes

WINTER, WEEK 12

from CHRIST THE LORD IS RISEN TODAY

Lives again our glorious King; Alleluia!
Where, O death, is now thy sting? Alleluia!
Once He died our souls to save; Alleluia!
Where thy victory, O grave? Alleluia!

Hail, the Lord of earth and heav'n; Alleluia!
Praise to Thee by both be giv'n; Alleluia!
Thee we greet triumphant now; Alleluia!
Hail, the Resurrection, Thou! Alleluia!

~ Charles Wesley

ੲ COPYBOOK & DICTATION

See _A Note About Names Referring to the Trinity_ in the Copybook section of Pedagogy and Practice.

In the Day 1 copywork, we again have _heaven_ shortened to _heav'n_ and _given_ shortened to _giv'n_. Refer to _Primer One Autumn_ Week 4 Teaching Notes for an explanation.

ੲ SPELLING, GRAMMAR, AND WORD USAGE

Day 1 _Writing Sentences_

Answers (examples): Easter usually falls in March or April. February is sometimes cold and snowy. My brother Ethan plays the piano.

Day 2 *Rhyming Words*
Answers (will vary): strays, prays, raise, maze, maize, craze, phrase; how, plough, plow, bow, bough, chow, meow

CR NATURE STUDY
Birds See Winter Week 7 Nature Study Teaching Notes.

PRIMER ONE SPRING
TEACHING NOTES & HELPS

THE SWING

How do you like to go up in a swing,
Up in the air so blue?
Oh, I do think it the pleasantest thing
Ever a child can do!

Up in the air and over the wall,
Till I can see so wide,
Rivers and trees and cattle and all
Over the countryside—

Till I look down on the garden green,
Down on the roof so brown
Up in the air I go flying again,
Up in the air and down!

~ Robert Louis Stevenson

℃ COPYBOOK & DICTATION

Review the instructions for Copybook and for Dication in the Pedagogy & Practice section of the Introduction.

℃ SPELLING, GRAMMAR, AND WORD USAGE

Review the instructions for Spelling, Grammar, and Word Usage in the Pedagogy & Practice section of the Introduction.

Note that the first letter of each line of poetry is capitalized.

Day 1 *Writing Sentences* As students write sentences this week using color words, remind them that every sentence starts with a capital letter and ends with end punctuation.

Day 2 *Making Plurals* Talk with students about other plural words that are formed by an internal change in the word. See if they can think of some words like this. Examples might include: *man (men); tooth (teeth); foot (feet); woman (women); goose (geese)*. A few words have no change at between the singular and plural forms, like *sheep*. Ask students to think of others. Examples: *dust, deer, celery, furniture, spaghetti.*

Day 4 Compound Words
Compound word in this week's selection: countryside. *Examples of other compound words:* weekday, inside, rooftop, riverboat, newsstand, ladybug

CR NATURE STUDY

> *"The only right way to begin plant study with young children is through awakening their interest in and love for flowers. Most children love flowers naturally..."* ~ Anna Bostford Comstock, Handbook of Nature Study

Review the instructions for Nature Study in the Pedagogy & Practice section of the Introduction.

The study of plants is called **botany.** Begin by talking with students about the differences between plants and animals. What are the characteristics that plants and animals share? *(alive, growing, need nourishment, reproduce)* How are plants different from animals? *(plants generally stay in one spot; can make their own food; have no sensory organs - eyes, ears, etc.)* Animals and plants are dependent on each other in many ways. Plants help animals to live. They provide food, shelter, and clothing, among other things. Plants need carbon dioxide to produce their food, and in the process they give off oxygen. Animals need this oxygen to breathe, and in the process of respiration give off carbon dioxide, which plants need to produce their food. So the cycle goes. Help students appreciate this marvelous design.

As an ongoing project beginning this week, students are instructed to plant flower seeds. Each week, they will be prompted to observe the growth of the plants and sketch what they see on the Plant Growth chart in the Appendix of *Primer One Spring*.

To plant seeds, you will need:

* a small pot with a drainage hole at the bottom, and a saucer underneath
* some medium size rocks (driveway gravel works well)
* potting soil
* flower or vegetable seeds (choose ones with a quick germination time - check the package)

Put the rocks in the bottom third of the pot. This will allow water to drain but will keep the soil in. Fill the pot with dirt, leaving about 3/4 in. at the top. Take the seeds out of the package, and observe them with students. Look at the size, the shape, and the color. Are they hard or soft? If the seeds are larger, try cutting one open and observing it. Before you plant the seeds, have students draw a picture of them in the first frame of the Plant Growth chart (Appendix, *Primer One Spring*).

Place a few of the remaining intact seeds on top of the

soil, spacing them an inch or so apart. Press them into the soil to the depth indicated on the package. Then, water the seeds in the pot and place it in a sunny windowsill or on your back porch, if it is warm enough. Remember to water the growing plants a little each day, but be careful not to over-water. Most seed packages will have instructions for how to water and care for those particular seedlings.

In addition to observing and charting plant growth, students will conduct some simple experiments with the young plants over the next few weeks.

This week, students are instructed to study the parts of a flower. Use the links on the You may purchase this on the *Primer Resources Webpage* to find illustrations and explanations. Help students to identify and begin to learn the purpose of these plant flower parts: **stem, fruit, leaf, flower, seed, roots.** For the activity in the workbook, either have students draw and label the parts of the flower, or print out an illustration from one of the links and cut and paste it into the box on Day 2.

Beginning in Week 2, students will choose a flower each week to observe and learn about. Choose any of the flowers which you can find in your backyard, park, along a trail, or in a meadow. Any flower will do, even those which some may consider a weed.

SPRING, WEEK 2

from THE TALE OF BENJAMIN BUNNY

They went away hand in hand, and got upon the flat top of the wall at the bottom of the wood. From here they looked down into Mr. McGregor's garden. Peter's shoes and coat were plainly to be seen upon the scarecrow, topped with an old tam-o-shanter of Mr. McGregor's.

Little Benjamin said, "It spoils people's clothes to squeeze under a gate; the proper way to get in, is to climb down a pear tree."

Peter fell down head first; but it was of no consequence, as the bed below was newly raked and quite soft.

It had been sown with lettuces.

They left a great many odd little foot-marks all over the bed, especially little Benjamin, who was wearing clogs.

~ Beatrix Potter

∝ COPYBOOK & DICTATION
Make sure students carefully observe where the punctuation and capitalization are placed.

Note that the first word of each paragraph of prose is indented. In typeset, you will sometimes see paragraphs that are not indented when they are separated by a line, as in this book. Show this to students, but always have them indent when they are writing by hand.

∝ SPELLING, GRAMMAR, AND WORD USAGE
Day 1 *Possessive Forms* After students have identified the possessive names in the selection, ask them what belongs to Mr. McGregor in the selection (*garden, tam-o-shanter*), and what belongs to Peter (*shoes and coat*).

78

Day 2 *Making Plurals* In order to help students remember which words use **-es** when making plurals, have them listen the the end of the root word. If it ends in /**ch**/, /**sh**/, /**x**/, /**s**/, and /**z**/, it will probably require an **-es**. We say that if the root word *hisses,* add **-es**. Review words that form plurals by changing internally or by no change from the singular form.

Answers: Names used as possessives in the selection: Mr. McGregor's, Peter's. Compound word in today's selection: scarecrow

Day 2 *Making Plurals*
Answers: people *or* persons; shoes, churches, teeth, gates, watches; men, trees, fish *or* fishes

Day 3 *Possesive Forms: Plural* When writing a plural possessive, sometimes the noun possessed will need to be made plural as well. Ask students if they notice any plural nouns that do not change from the singular in this list (honey *is the same in both plural and singular forms; and the crickets all together may make a collective* chirp *rather than individual* chirps).

Answers: rabbits' coats, gardens' walls, bees' honey; crickets' chirp or crickets' chirps, birds' wings

Day 4 *Homonyms* Have students use both forms orally in a sentence to make sure they understand the difference in meanings.

Answers: shoo, weigh, sow *and* so, rose (*can be the flower or the act of standing up*), I or aye, eight

79

❧ NATURE STUDY

Choose a flower for study and observation each week. Talk with students and choose ones they would like to study. Co-op teachers may assign different flowers to individual students each week, and ask students to present their observations in the next class.

If you do not have immediate access to plants for observation, consider checking out books from the library or finding online resources to view and learn about specific flowers. Check the You may purchase this on the *Primer Resources Webpage* for links and resources to help with this.

The goal of these lessons is for students to simply observe a plant and talk about it with you. Review the parts of the plant they learned in Week 1, and then see if they can identify each one on their plant of the week, giving them plenty of help as needed. Do not worry if they cannot find all the parts or talk about every point listed; these are just a guide to help the observation and discussion.

Students are also prompted to draw what is happening to their flower seeds each week.

The seed package should indicate how big the plants need to be before they are transplanted outdoors or into a bigger pot, and how far apart to plant the seedlings. Students can enjoy their flowers for the entire summer.

Optional Enrichment Activities (see the *Primer Resources Webpage* for links and resources to help with these activities):

◆ Learn new techniques, such as watercolor or chalk

80

for drawing or painting plants. Watercolors are an excellent medium to learn.

◆ Plan and plant a vegetable or flower garden.

SPRING, WEEK 3

from PROVERBS

My son, do not forget my law,
   but let your heart keep my commands;
   for length of days and long life
   and peace they will add to you.

Let not mercy and truth forsake you;
   bind them around your neck,
   write them on the tablet of your heart,
   and so find favor and high esteem
   in the sight of God and man.

Trust in the Lord with all your heart,
   and lean not on your own understanding;
   in all your ways acknowledge Him,
   and He shall direct your paths.

~ Proverbs 3:1-6, New King James Versionn

☙ COPYBOOK & DICTATION

See *A Note About Scripture Copybook Selections* and *A Note About Names Referring to the Trinity* in the Copybook section of Pedagogy and Practice.

ℭℛ Spelling, Grammar, and Word Usage

Day 1 *Contractions*
Answers: let's, they'll, He'll, haven't, you're

Day 2 *Rhyming Words*
Answers (will vary): start, part, chart, smart, apart; height, fight, blight, flight, excite, delight; rind, mind, signed, grind, designed, unwind, confined

Day 3 *Possessive Forms*
Answers (examples): your heart, our minds, his love, its path, their ways

Day 4 *Homonyms*
Answers (examples): Please walk your dog. You're my favorite teacher.

ℭℛ Nature Study
Plants See Weeks 1-2 Spring Nature Study Teaching Notes.

Spring, Week 4

from The Miracle

The next day was foggy. Everything on the farm was dripping wet. The grass looked like a magic carpet. The asparagus patch looked like a silver forest.

On foggy mornings, Charlotte's web was truly a thing of beauty. This morning each thin strand was decorated with dozens of tiny beads of water. The web glistened in the light and made a pattern of loveliness and mystery, like a delicate veil. Even Lurvy, who wasn't particularly interested in beauty, noticed the web when he came with the pig's breakfast. He noted how clearly it showed up and he noted how big and carefully built it was. And then he took another look and he saw something that made him set his pail down.

~ *Charlotte's Web*, by E.B. White

ᴄꞬ Sᴘᴇʟʟɪɴɢ, Gʀᴀᴍᴍᴀʀ, ᴀɴᴅ Wᴏʀᴅ Usᴀɢᴇ

Day 1 *Similes* Instruct students to look for the words *like* or *as* to recognize **similes**. (*Than* sometimes indicates a simile, but it is easier to concentrate on *like* and *as* for now.) Not every use of these words indicate a simile. Sometimes *like* or *as* are used to compare things of the same nature, and these uses do not indicate a simile. Examples of this include: *My sister looks like me. The boy was almost as tall as his father.*

Similes are very often used after a form of *be* or some other verb that indicates **seeming** or **becoming** (for example: *feel, smell, sound, look, appear, became, or grew*). Be on the lookout for similes you can point out when you read aloud and in students' other subjects.

Answers: grass *is compared to* a magic carpet; asparagus patch *is compared to* a silver forest

Day 2 *Adding Suffixes:* y *changing to* i Remind students that when **y** is part of a phongram team (vowel digraph) at the end of the word, the **y** will not change to **i**. Watch for **ay, oy, ey.**

Answers: loveliness, beautiful, foggier, crying, earlier, joyful

Day 3 *Possessive Forms*
Answers: web's beauty, Charlotte's web, pigs' breakfast,

83

Lurvy's pail;

Day 3 *Similes*
Answer: the pattern of the web *is compared to* a veil

Day 4 *Homonyms* Have students use both forms orally in a sentence to make sure they understand the difference in meanings.

Answers: vale (usually refers to a valley); pale, hour;

Day 4 *Rhyming Words*
Answers (will vary): hail, mail, sale, stale, trail, braille; bleed, lead, weed, steed, agreed, indeed

CR NATURE STUDY
Plants See Weeks 1-2 Spring Nature Study Teaching Notes.

For this week's experiment, have students skip a watering or two and observe the effects.

SPRING, WEEK 5
_____

PSALM 23

The Lord is my shepherd;
    I shall not want.
He makes me to lie down in green pastures;
    He leads me beside the still waters.
He restores my soul;
    He leads me in the paths of righteousness
    For His name's sake.

Yea, though I walk through the valley of the shadow of death,
    I will fear no evil;
    For You are with me;
    Your rod and Your staff, they comfort me.

You prepare a table before me in the presence of my enemies;
    You anoint my head with oil;
    My cup runs over.
Surely goodness and mercy shall follow me
    All the days of my life;
    And I will dwell in the house of the Lord
    Forever.

~ New King James Version

◌ COPYBOOK & DICTATION

See *A Note About Scripture Copybook Selections* and *A Note About Names Referring to the Trinity* in the Copybook section of Pedagogy and Practice.

◌ SPELLING, GRAMMAR, AND WORD USAGE

Day 1 *Possessive Forms*
Answers: righteousness' paths, sake of His name

Day 2 *Contractions*
Answers: I'll, I'll, he's, there's, she'd

Day 4 *Homonyms*
Answer: threw

◌ NATURE STUDY

Plants See Weeks 1-2 Spring Nature Study Teaching Notes.

For this week's experiment, ask students to notice the stem. Does it grow straight up or does it lean or turn? Plants will usually turn toward the light. Do not tell students this, show them. Have them observe what happens when you turn the plant away from the light (*it should start leaning toward the light again*).

SPRING, WEEK 6

THE FLOWERS

All the names I know from nurse:
Gardener's garters, Shepherd's purse,
Bachelor's buttons, Lady smock,
And the Lady Hollyhock.
Fairy places, fairy things,
Fairy woods where the wild bee wings,
Tiny trees for tiny dames –
These must all be fairy names!
Tiny woods below whose boughs
Shady fairies weave a house;
Tiny tree-tops, rose or thyme,
Where the braver fairies climb!
Fair are grown-up people's trees
But the fairest woods are these;
Where, if I were not so tall,
I should live for good and all.

~ Robert Louis Stevenson

ℛ SPELLING, GRAMMAR, AND WORD USAGE

Day 3 *Homonyms* Have students use both forms orally in a sentence to make sure they understand the difference in meanings.

Answers: eye or aye, no, fare, be, bows, time, four or fore

Day 4 Possessive Forms
Answers: Gardener's garters = garters of a gardener; shepherd's purse = purse of a shepherd; bachelor's buttons = buttons of a bachelor; people's trees = trees of people

CR NATURE STUDY

> *By the breath of God ice is given, and the broad waters are frozen. Also with moisture He saturates the thick clouds; He scatters His bright clouds. And they swirl about, being turned by His guidance, that they may do whatever He commands them on the face of the whole earth.* ~ *Job 37:10-12*

In bygone days, men and women who kept journals often noted the weather each day. When there was no air conditioning or heat, and certainly when life and livelihood depended on agriculture, the weather was a constant source of interest and concern.

For this week's lesson, learn about the different types of clouds. See links on the *Primer Resources Webpage* to excellent illustrations and explanations. Have students draw and label the four cloud types listed.

Additionally, for the next month, students should make note of the weather each day. A blank calendar for this purpose is included in the Appendix of *Primer One Spring.* Copy it onto cardstock and have students keep it out where they will see it and be reminded.

Decide together with students how to record the weather information, and any additional information to be recorded on their weather charts. Some suggestions:

- Sunny, cloudy, or rainy? Draw symbols for each.

- If you have a thermometer, record the temperature each morning, or any time of day. Try to record at the same time each day.

- Types of clouds seen in the sky.

SPRING, WEEK 7

from POOH INVENTS A NEW GAME AND EEYORE JOINS IN

By the time it came to the edge of the Forest, the stream had grown up, so that it was almost a river, and being grown-up, it did not run and jump and sparkle along as it used to do when it was younger, but moved more slowly. For it knew now where it was going, and it said to itself, "There is no hurry. We shall get there someday." But all the little streams higher up in the Forest went this way and that, quickly, eagerly, having so much to find out before it was too late.

There was a broad track, almost as broad as a road, leading from the Outland to the Forest, but before it could come to the Forest, it had to cross this river. So, where it crossed, there was a wooden bridge, almost as broad as a road, with wooden rails on each side of it.

~ *The House at Pooh Corner*, by A.A. Milne

℞ COPYBOOK & DICTATION

A. A. Milne uses capitalization to show **personification** of the places, trees, and objects in Christopher Robin's world. He gives living qualities or characteristics of persons to the *Sun*, the *Pine Trees*, and even to the *Very Deep Pit*. Christopher Robin speaks of the Forest and Outland as proper place names because to him there is only ONE Forest and only ONE Outland. Personification will be discussed at length in future books. Rather than pointing out the capitalization of these objects, let students notice this (or not!) Let them ask you about the rules if it occurs to them. If not, let it pass. Proper nouns and capitalization will be covered in *Primer Two*.

℞ Spelling, Grammar, and Word Usage

Day 1 *Writing Book Titles* When a book title written in typeface (in books, articles, papers, etc,), it will usually be italicized, or de-italicized if the rest of the sentence is already in italics. Examples: *Winnie-the-Pooh* by A.A. Milne OR Winnie-the-Pooh *by A.A. Milne.*

Day 2 *Could, Should, Would*
Answers: wouldn't, couldn't, shouldn't

Day 4 *Homonyms*
Answers: two *and* too, buy *and* bye, new, hi, sew *and* sow, rode *and* rowed, would

℞ Nature Study

Learn about the water cycle—another evidence of how the world is intricately designed for our comfort and enjoyment. See links on the *Primer Resources Webpage* for explanations and illustrations.

For the activity, draw a simplified scheme of the water cycle on the whiteboard for the students to copy.

SPRING, WEEK 8

from THE CICADA

The Common Cicada likes to lay her eggs on small dry branches. She chooses, as far as possible, tiny stalks, which may be of any size between that of a straw and a lead-pencil. The sprig is never lying on the ground, is usually nearly upright in position, and is almost always dead.

Having found a twig to suit her, she makes a row of pricks with the sharp instrument on her chest — such pricks as might be made with a pin if it were driven downwards on a slant, so as to tear the fibres and force them slightly upwards. If she is undisturbed she will make thirty or forty of these pricks on the same twig.

In the tiny cells formed by these pricks she lays her eggs. The cells are narrow passages, each one slanting down towards the one below it. I generally find about ten eggs in each cell, so it is plain that the Cicada lays between three and four hundred eggs altogether.

~ *Fabre's Book of Insects*, by Jean-Henri Fabre

℘ SPELLING, GRAMMAR, AND WORD USAGE

Day 2 *Rhyming Words*

Answers (will vary): whig, pig, wig, sprig; best, blessed, guest, quest, jest, dressed, arrest; aunt, ant, can't, chant, scant

Day 3 *Writing Numbers*

Answers: 100; 1,000; 1,000,000; five hundred, eight thousand, two million

Day 4 *Antonyms*
Answers (examples): wet; large *or* huge; dull; alive; air *or* sky; up; far; wide *or* broad

ℭ℞ NATURE STUDY

Insects are fascinating creatures, fun to watch and full of wonderful lessons for our lives. Although some insects are harmful to man, almost all insects have some specific purpose in our world. (I must admit I am still waiting to find out the purpose of mosquitos and ticks—both of which abound in Virginia.)

There are a few tools which, though not required, will make the collection and observation of insects a bit easier. Among the most helpful are a bug viewer with a magnifying lens and a butterfly net. See links on the *Primer Resources Webpage* for inexpensive versions of these. You will no doubt be able to find many books with fascinating information and pictures at your local library.

Do not neglect the practice of simply going outside and watching a bug. It is amazing how very still a normally wiggly student can sit while watching a busy ant carrying food. Caution students not to touch insects, as many do sting and some are poisonous.

Study the characteristics of an insect with students. Find a picture illustrating these characteristics in a book or on the field guide link from the *Primer Resources Webpage*.

✓ ***Insects do not have a backbone, but have an*** **exoskeleton.**
   Exo- means *outside.* The skeleton of an insect is outside of its body. Because insects do not have backbones,

91

they are called **invertebrates.** Discuss with students how insects differ from fish, mammals, birds, and reptiles, all of which have backbones.

✓ *Insects have three main body parts:* **head, thorax, and abdomen.** Find a picture illustrating this, either in a book or from the field guide link on the You may purchase this on the *Primer Resources Webpage.*

✓ *Insects have a pair of* **antennae on their heads.** *Antennae* is plural; the singular form is **antenna.**

✓ *Insects have three pairs of legs.*

✓ *Insects have two pairs of wings.*

Examples of insects include: *fly, mosquito, tick, ant, grasshopper, bee, wasp, dragonfly, gnat, flea, cricket, butterfly, praying mantis,* and *moth.*

If students mention spiders, tell them that spiders are not insects, but are a separate class of animals called **arachnids.** Spiders have eight legs, no wings, and no antennae.

What about worms? Why aren't they insects? Compare the characteristics of a worm with the list above to see.

SPRING, WEEK 9
_____

THE WORM

When the earth is turned in spring
The worms are fat as anything.
And birds come flying all around

To eat the worms right off the ground.
They like worms just as much as I
Like bread and milk and apple pie.
And once, when I was very young,
I put a worm right on my tongue.
I didn't like the taste a bit,
And so I didn't swallow it.
But oh, it makes my mother squirm
Because she thinks I ate that worm!

~ by Ralph Bergengren

ℭℛ Spelling, Grammar, and Word Usage

Day 2 Contractions
Answers: didn't, haven't, isn't, don't, won't (related to *would*)

Day 3 Possessive Forms
Answers: my tongue, my mother, birds' beaks, your apple pie, her bread, worms' bodies

Day 4 Synonyms
Answers (examples): ground, world; plump; little; heavens; singing; tiny; huge, great

ℭℛ Nature Study

Each week, students are directed to choose an insect to observe, discuss, and draw. As always, it is best to have students observe and identify the actual insects which live in your geographical area if at all possible. Remind students not to touch insects. As needed, use field guides, books, and online resources to study, observe, and identify. See links on the *Primer Resources Webpage*.

Optional Enrichment (links to resources for all of these ideas are on the *Primer Resources Webpage*):

* Set up and observe an ant farm.
* Watch caterpillars change from to cocoon to butterflies in a butterfly garden.

SPRING, WEEK 10

from HOW THE RHINOCEROS GOT HIS SKIN

And the Rhinoceros did. He buttoned it up with the three buttons, and it tickled like cake crumbs in bed. Then he wanted to scratch, but that made it worse; and then he lay down on the sands and rolled and rolled and rolled, and every time he rolled the cake crumbs tickled him worse and worse and worse. Then he ran to the palm-tree and rubbed and rubbed and rubbed himself against it. He rubbed so much and so hard that he rubbed his skin into a great fold over his shoulders, and another fold underneath, where the buttons used to be (but he rubbed the buttons off), and he rubbed some more folds over his legs. And it spoiled his temper, but it didn't make the least difference to the cake-crumbs. They were inside his skin and they tickled. So he went home, very angry indeed and horribly scratchy; and from that day to this every rhinoceros has great folds in his skin and a very bad temper, all on account of the cake-crumbs inside.

~ *Just So Stories*, by Rudyard Kiplingn

SPELLING, GRAMMAR, AND WORD USAGE

Day 1 *Similes* Finding the simile in the selection might be a little tricky. First, have students find the word *like*. Ask them what is the *it* which is doing the tickling? If they have trouble, give a hint to look at the title of the chapter on this week's copybook selection.

Answers: the way the rhinoceros' skin tickles is compared to cake crumbs (*I know this probably never happens in your house, but think what it WOULD feel like IF you had crumbs inside your clothes or on your bed.*)

Day 2 *Synonyms*
Answers (examples): rubbed, hard, great, spoiled, temper

Day 3 *Antonyms*
Answers (examples): down; gently; tiny or small; under; rotten or nasty; hate; cold; outside

Day 4 *Rhyming Words*
Answers (will vary): catch, match, snatch, attach; boar, chore, store, four, door, war, before; beast, east, greased, priest, released; berry, bury (*depending on dialect*), dairy, marry, prairie, canary

℞ NATURE STUDY
Insects See Weeks 8-9 Spring Nature Study Teaching Notes.

SPRING, WEEK 11

from MY COUNTRY, 'TIS OF THEE

My country, 'tis of thee,
Sweet land of liberty,
Of thee I sing;
Land where my fathers died,
Land of the Pilgrims' pride,
From every mountainside
Let freedom ring.

My native country, thee,

Land of the noble free—
Thy name I love
I love thy rocks and rills
Thy woods and templed hills
My heart with rapture thrills
Like that above.

~ Samuel Francis Smith

ℂ SPELLING, GRAMMAR, AND WORD USAGE

On Day 1, after students find the possessive form using an apostrophe in the selection, ask if they can find the possessives in the selection which use 'of' (land of liberty, land of the Pilgrim's pride). Note that 'of thee' is not a possessive here, since thee is not possessed, but is sung of. If students are confused by this, show how the verse could be rewritten as 'I sing of (about) thee'.

Day 1 *Synonyms & Possessive Forms*

Answers: country *and* land *are synonyms;* liberty *and* freedom *are synonyms;* Pilgrim's pride = pride of the Pilgrims.

Day 2 *Possessive Forms*

Answers: My native country, land of the noble free, Thy name, thy rocks and rills, thy woods and templed hills, my heart

ℂ NATURE STUDY

Insects See Weeks 8-9 Spring Nature Study Teaching Notes.

SPRING, WEEK 12

from MY COUNTRY, 'TIS OF THEE

Let music swell the breeze,
And ring from all the trees
Sweet freedom's song;
Let mortal tongues awake
Let all that breathe partake,
Let rocks their silence break—
The sound prolong.

Our fathers' God, to Thee,
Author of liberty,
To Thee we sing;
Long may our land be bright
With freedom's holy light;
Protect us by Thy might,
Great God, our King.

~ Samuel Francis Smith

‍ COPYBOOK & DICTATION

See *A Note About Scripture Copybook Selections* and *A Note About Names Referring to the Trinity* in the Copybook section of Pedagogy and Practice.

‍ SPELLING, GRAMMAR, AND WORD USAGE

Day 1 *Rhyming Words*

Answers (will vary): cheese, bees, seas, sneeze, tease, these; bride, beside, guide, cried, tried, outside

Day 2 *Possessive Forms*

Answers: Our father's God = the God of our fathers (*note both our and father's are possessive*); author of liberty = liberty's author; freedom's light = light of freedom; Thy might = might of Thee; our King = King of us

Day 4 *Antonyms*
Answers (examples): enslaved, bound, expensive; none, few; asleep; noise; short, brief; dull, dim; dark

ᘓ NATURE STUDY
Insects See Weeks 8-9 Spring Nature Study Teaching Notes.

APPENDIX

The phonics and spelling rules reviewed in *Primer Two* are listed below, along with the lesson(s) where these rules are reviewed. This is not intended to be an exhaustive list of phonics & spelling rules, nor are they introduced in any particular order, but are introduced as they occur in literary selections. It is expected that all Primer students are concurrently studying a comprhensive phonics and spelling course.

LETTER & PHONOGRAM SOUNDS

* The letter **c** always says /**s**/ before **e, i,** or **y.** The letter **g** may say /**j**/ before **e, i,** or **y.** *(Winter Week 10)*

* Words that say /**ā**/ at the end usually end in **ay.** If a word ends with **a,** it usually says /**ah**/. *(Autumn Week 1)*

* The phonogram **dge** says /**j**/ at the end of a word. The **e** is silent. *(Winter Week 4)*

* The phonogram **ea** can say /**ē**/ as in *tea,* /**ĕ**/ as in *bread,* or /**ā**/ as in *steak. (Autumn Week 4)*

* The phonogram **ee** says /**ē**/. *(Autumn Week 12)*

* The phonograms **er** as in *her,* **ir** as in *first,* **ur** as in *church,* **ear** as in *early,* and **or** used after **w** as in *worships* all make the sound /**er**/. *(Winter Weeks 9 & 11, Spring Week 9)*

* The phonogram **ew** can say /**oo**/ as in *few. (Winter Week 7)*

* The phonogram **igh** says /**ī**/. *(Autumn Week 3)*

* The phonogram **oo** can say /**oo**/ as in *food,* /**oo**/ as in *book,* /**ō**/ as in *floor,* and /**ŭ**/ as in *blood. (Autumn Week 10, Winter Week 7)*

* The phonogram **or** usually says /**er**/ when it comes after

w. *(Autumn Week 3)*

* The phonogram **ou** can say /**ow**/ as in *shout*, /ō/ as in *four*, or /**oo**/ as in *soup*, or /ŭ/ as in *young*. *(Autumn Week 5, Winter Week 7)*

* The phonogram **ow** can say /**ow**/ as in cow, or /ō/ as in *snow*. *(Autumn Week 6)*

Spelling Rules & Tips

* Use **i** before **e**, except after **c**, and when it says /ā/ as in *neighbor*. There are a few exceptions which should be memorized: *either, neither, height, seize, leisure, foreign, sovereign, counterfeit, protein, weird* *(Winter Week 5)*

* The sound /k/ can be spelled with the two letter phonogram **ck**, but only after a short vowel. The phonogram **ck** is never used at the beginning of a word, after long vowels, or after vowel teams. *(Spring Week 6)*

* **y** is sometimes used as a vowel, saying /ĭ/, /ī/, or /ē/. Words that end in with the single vowel **-y** *(not a vowel digraph)* usually exchange the **y** for an **i** when a suffix is added to the word, unless the suffix begins with a **i**. *(Spring Week 4)*

* The phonogram **oi** cannot be used at the end of a word because English words do not end in **i**. Use **oy** at the end of a word, and sometimes in the middle. *(Autumn Week 9)*

* The phonogram **ou** in *could, would,* and *should* says /**oo**/ as in *book*, and the **l** is silent. *(Spring Week 7)*

* Most names of persons, places, things, or ideas are made plural (more than one) by adding **-s** or **-es** to the base word. In some words ending in **f**, the **f** changes to

v and then you add **-es**. Example: leaf, change **f** → **v** + **-es** = leaves. Some words have an internal change, like *mice*, and some words have no change at all, like *dust*. *(Autumn Week 2, Spring Weeks 1 & 2)*

• The suffix indicating the past tense is **-ed**. It says /d/ or /t/ unless the base word ends in **-d** or **-t**, in which case it says /ed/. Sometimes the past tense is formed by totally changing the word. Example: *have* → *had* *(Autumn, Week 2)*

• To add a suffix that begins with a vowel to a one-syllable word, double the final consonant IF the word ends in one vowel followed by one consonant that you can see AND hear. *(Autumn Week 5)*

• Words that end with a silent **-e** drop the **e** when a suffix that begins with a vowel is added. *(Autumn Week 7)*

• *Would, could,* and *should* use the **ou** phonogram to say /ŭ/. The **l** is silent. The root word for *would* is *will, should* is *shall,* and *could* is *can.* *(Winter Week 8)*

• Compound words are made by joining two whole words. *(Spring Week 1)*

• When *full* is added to another word to make a new compound word, it is spelled with just one **l**. *(Autumn Week 7)*

• An **apostrophe** (') **+** s is added to a word to show possession. *(Spring Week 2)*

• To form the possessive of plural words ending in **-s**, add the **apostrophe** (') alone after the **-s.** *(Spring Week 2)*

• A **contraction** shortens a group of words by replacing a letter or letters with an **apostrophe** ('). *(Winter Week 8, Spring Week 3)*

GRAMMAR & WORD USAGE

• Names of particular persons, places, or things begin with a capital letter. *(Winter Week 3)*

• Possessive pronouns do not need an added **'s,** such as *my, our, your, his, her, its,* and *their. (Spring Week 3)*

• The first letter of a title used as part of a name is capitalized. *(Winter Week 3)*

• Capitalize the first letter of the month when writing a date. Place a comma between the day and the year. *(Winter Week 3)*

• In general, write words in a series with commas between each item in the series, using *and* only before the last item in the series. *(Winter Week 9)*

• Underline book titles and capitalize all of the important words. *(Spring Week 7)*

• Enclose chapter titles with quotation marks and capitalize all of the important words. *(Spring Week 7)*

• Enclose poems and song titles with quotation marks and capitalize all of the important words. *(Spring Week 11)*

• **Homonyms** are words that sound the same, but have different spellings and meanings. *Dear* and *deer* are homonyms. *(Winter Week 11, Spring Week 1)*

• **Antonyms** are words that have opposite meanings, like *happy* and *sad. (Spring Week 8)*

• **Synonyms** are words that have similar meanings, like *happy* and *glad. (Spring Week 9)*

FIGURES OF SPEECH

• A **simile** compares two things that are not usually

associated with one another by using the words *like, as,* or *than. (Spring Week 4)*

Beginning Consonant Blends for Rhyming

th, sh, ch, wh, pr, tr, gr, br, cr, dr, fr, st, sp, sk, sc, sw, sm, sn, pl, cl, bl, fl, sl, gl, tw, str, spl, spr

NOTES

NOTES

NOTES

Made in the USA
Monee, IL
03 August 2020

37268535R00066